Wonders of **CHINA**

Lynn M. Stone

The Rourke Book Company, Inc.
Vero Beach, Florida 32964

PHOTO CREDITS
© Keren Su: all photos except p. 15 © Frank Balthis

Library of Congress Cataloging-in-Publication Data

Stone, Lynn M.
    Wonders of China / Lynn M. Stone.
        p. cm. — (China)
    Includes index.
    ISBN 1-55916-322-4
    1. China—Juvenile literature. [1. China] I. Title.

DS706 .S796 2000
951—dc21

00–039005

Printed in the USA

CONTENTS

WONDERS OF CHINA

China is an **ancient** country with many **cultures** between its wide borders. It is a land of rugged mountains, deserts, plains, forests, canyons, and shores. But it is also a land of temples, tombs, statues, gardens, palaces, pottery, and an amazing Great Wall.

Some of China's wonders are the works of people from many cultures. Others are natural, the wonderful works of nature's forces. This book will describe some of each.

The ancient Silk Road, a famous trade route, travels along many old wonders, including Lake Karakuli on China's Pamir Plateau.

THE GREAT WALL

China's Great Wall is an almost unbelievable structure. It stretches across more than 3,750 miles (6,000 kilometers) like a giant serpent of stone.

Amazingly, most of the Great Wall was built 2,500 years ago! In 1368, China's rulers began to build additions to the wall. That project lasted about 200 years. The wall looks now just as it did then.

The wall begins at the Jiaya Pass in Gansu Province in the west. It reaches eastward to the mouth of the Yalu River in Liaoning Province.

The wall was built to keep out tribes from the north. It has battle forts built into it.

China's legendary Great Wall was built as a defense against invaders from the north.

The Badaling section of the Great Wall is northwest of Beijing, China's capital. The wall there averages 26 feet (8 meters) in height and 19 feet (6 meters) in width.

Much smaller walls contain the Forbidden City in Beijing.

BEIJING'S WONDERS

Beijing's Forbidden City is one of the city's outstanding places. It was the home of China's emperors from 1420 to 1924. The Forbidden City is actually a series of halls, marble floors, red walls, and golden rooftops. It was called the Forbidden City because it was open only to the rulers of China.

Nearby is the Temple of Heaven. It is, in fact, several temples and altars in a park setting.

A rainbow rises over Beijing's
Heavenly Temple.

It's not Arizona, but, rather the amazing limestone Stone Forest in Kunming.

The jagged peaks of Mt. Huangshan glow in the late day clouds in Anhui Province.

LONGMEN CAVES

For some 400 years, **Buddhist** craftsmen worked to make the **sculptures** known as the Longmen Caves. These sculptures, or carvings, were begun in the year 494.

Many of the Longmen Cave sculptures are of human figures. They are carved into the rock cliffs of the Yi River near Luoyang in Henan Province.

The Buddhist religion was brought to China from India long ago. China has many Buddhist holy places.

Buddhist sculptures appear in the Longmen cliff caves along the Yi River in Henan Province.

POTALA PALACE

China has many wonderful old palaces. The Potala Palace, built in the 1600's is one of the best known.

The Potala Palace is on a hill overlooking the city of Lhasa. Lhasa is high in the mountains of Tibet.

The palace has a white section which rises in huge steps to a red section. Visitors are allowed into only a small part of the palace.

The Potala Palace is the main landmark of Lhasa in Tibet.

TERRACOTTA ARMY

The Chinese emperor who died about 2,200 years ago near the city of Xi'an wasn't buried alone.

Near the emperor's tomb, Chinese sculptors carved an army of **terracotta** soldiers. Terracotta is a hard material made by baking clay.

The hundreds of larger-than-life soldiers were supposed to guard the emperor. They did, until they were found by well diggers in 1974.

The terracotta soldiers still have their metal weapons, including poison-tipped arrows!

The emperor's Terracotta Army has stood at attention in Xi'an for more than 2,000 years.

THE THREE GORGES

Among China's natural wonders is the Yangtze River and its famous Three Gorges. The long, fast-flowing Yangtze and the smaller rivers that flow into it have many **gorges**.

Gorges are deep, narrow canyons. The Three Gorges area of the Yangtze covers 125 miles (200 kilometers) in central China.

The first of the Three Gorges has stone walls rising 4,000 feet (1,200 meters) from the river's banks.

A tour boat motors down the Yangtze River in the Three Gorges region.

MOUNT HUANGSHAN

Mountains cover much of China, but Mount Huangshan in Anhui Province is a favorite.

Mount Huangshan, also called Yellow Mountain, has several sharp peaks. They have poetic names like Lotus Flower, Purple Cloud, and Peach Blossom. Chinese artists have always been impressed by the mountain's peaks and changing moods.

People can hike the 6,000-foot (1,800-meter) mountain and stay at guest houses on the peaks.

GLOSSARY

ancient (AYN shent) — very old

Buddhist (BOO dist) — one who practices Buddhism, a major religion of the East

culture (KUL chur) — the special ways in which a certain group of people live; the beliefs, customs, language, and other characteristics of a group

sculpture (SKULP chur) — a carved figure, usually of a person or animal

terracotta (TAIR uh KAH tuh) — hard, baked clay with a rusty color

FURTHER INFORMATION

Find out more about the wonders of China and China in general with these helpful bodies and information sites:

- Hamilton, Jill. *The Visual Dictionary of Ancient Civilizations*. Dorling Kindersley, 1994
- McNeese, Tim. *The Great Wall of China*. Lucent, 1997
- Nicholson, Robert. *Ancient China*. Chelsea House, 1993
- Patent, Dorothy Hinshaw Patent. *The Incredible Story of China's Buried Warriors*. Marshall Cavendish, 2000

China on-line at www.mytravelguide.com
Lonely Planet-Destination China on-line at www.lonelyplanet.com

INDEX